James Bunker Congdon

Quaker Quiddities

Friends in Council

.

James Bunker Congdon

Quaker Quiddities
Friends in Council

ISBN/EAN: 9783337408343

Printed in Europe, USA, Canada, Australia, Japan

Cover: Foto ©Lupo / pixelio.de

More available books at **www.hansebooks.com**

QUAKER QUIDDITIES;

OR,

FRIENDS IN COUNCIL

𝔄 Colloquy.

(*J. B. Congdon*)

The primal duties shine aloft — like stars;
The charities that soothe and heal and bless
Are scattered at the feet of man — like flowers.

THE EXCURSION.

BOSTON:

CROSBY, NICHOLS, LEE, AND COMPANY

117, WASHINGTON STREET.

1860.

BOSTON:

PRINTED BY JOHN WILSON AND SON

22, School Street.

𝔇𝔢𝔡𝔦𝔠𝔞𝔱𝔢𝔡 𝔱𝔬 𝔱𝔥𝔢 𝔄𝔩𝔲𝔪𝔫𝔦

OF THE

YEARLY-MEETING SCHOOL,

PROVIDENCE,

BY AN UNDERGRADUATE.

PREFACE.

THE following pages are given to the public without the sanction of the Meeting for Sufferings. Had the manuscript been submitted to the censorship of that body, it is hardly probable that its publication would have been *suffered.*

The course I have taken being contrary to discipline, I have thought it proper to send out my little book without the writer's name on the titlepage. I have no fear of disownment, should I be known as the offender. My age would prevent that; as, in the eye of the law, I am still an infant: but I am by no means sure that a punishment more in accordance with schoolroom usages would not follow.

I hope no one who reads what I have written will receive an impression that there is a shade of disrespect intended towards the Society of Friends. A member by birthright, my associations with them have always been of the most intimate character. I respect them as a body. I have, from conviction, adopted their princi-

ples ; and many if not most of their usages have, in my
opinion, the sanction of experience and sound reason.
But, although I am an undergraduate, I am old enough
to think and judge for myself. In the colloquy which
follows, some of my thoughts and opinions are re-
corded.

What is contained in the following pages has nothing
to do with *prize-essayism.* After it was written, I was
surprised to learn that the hundred-guinea offer had
produced a baker's dozen of books, each one of which
was considered by the writer conclusive as an answer
to the question, " Why is Quakerism declining ? " As
near as I can find out by a cursory examination of these
" essays to do " the hundred-guinea job successfully, Quakerism is declining because it is Quakerism, and not Epis-
copalianism, Methodism, or Mormonism. " Most lame
and impotent conclusion ! " one is prompted to exclaim,
in view of the result of this speculative operation in the
article of Quakerism. There is a decrease of the number of names on the rolls of the monthly meetings ; and
why ? Why ? because Quakerism is not Mormonism :
if it were, the number would increase.

The only questions which have any vitality in them,
connected with the admitted fact of the decline of Quakerism, are, "Is it worth saving ? " " Can it be saved ? "

"How can it be saved?" One thing is sure: it must show its right to a distinctive place in the world's civilization by something more significant and progressive than a formless method in its meetings and a uniform costume. Its negations cannot give it a longer lease of life. It must in some way grapple with the world, and show its potency by helping the world onward. The world is demanding aid from every organization that has for its object the inculcation of moral and religious truth. It is not satisfied, it should not be satisfied, with the plea of self-preservation. It seems to me that Quakerism is dying of isolation. But these questions are too mighty to be mooted in a preface to a pamphlet.

PROVIDENCE, R.I., 5mo. 21, 1860.

QUAKER QUIDDITIES.

FRIENDS IN COUNCIL.

Friends: SAMUEL BONUS *and* JEREMIAH AUSTEN.

JEREMIAH.

OH! this is mournful. Samuel, does thee know,
That, from our fathers' land beyond the sea, —
The land of FOX, of BARCLAY, and of PENN, —
Tidings have come of breaches wide and deep
In the defences which so long have kept
Our Zion safe and separate from the world?

SAMUEL.

A rumor reached me, that our Friends proposed,
In things of discipline, some little change.

JEREMIAH.

Some little change? Dost say, some little change?
A little change! The pillars twain, so long

The chief support of all our sect holds dear,
Are tottering to their fall.

SAMUEL.

My recent letters hardly give support
To such an apprehension. 'Twas supposed,
(Thus ran the tidings as they come to me,)
That by the favor of our weightiest Friends,
Who late in London held convening sage,
Some modes less rigid in our marriage rules
Might at the Annual Gathering be approved.
'Twas further rumored, that the same high source
Some trifling relaxation might ordain
In those requirings which restrain, so close,
Friends in the matters of attire and speech.

JEREMIAH.

Such is indeed the fact; and, knowing this,
Can thee the purposed consummation view
Without the deepest sadness and alarm?
To me it heralds overthrow and ruin.
The flood-gates open wide; the worldly waves
Rush unobstructed and relentless in,

And sweep before them every thing that gives,
To those who hold in purity our faith,
A place apart, distinctive and secure.

SAMUEL.

And can it be that our peculiar speech,
And vestments hued and fashioned by a rule
Made of an accident, with no support
But weak tradition, are the pillars strong,
Which give us all our beauty and our strength?
Are we by *these* distinctive and secure?
Are we defended from the world's array
By this environment of garb and speech?

JEREMIAH.

Mournful to me the saddening doubt implied
By thy bold questioning. Hear the holy word,
Bidding us not to this vain world conform,
But bear the daily cross, denying self;
Despising Fashion's *ignis fatuus* light, —
Dazzling* to blind, and leading to betray.

---

* See Note A.

SAMUEL.

Is this the measure of the word inspired, —
" Self to deny, the sacred cross to bear ; "
To fix the cut and color of a coat,
Use or misuse a certain form of speech,
Making that holy which is only odd ?

JEREMIAH.

" Be not conformed," the sacred page repeats ;
" But be ye transformed " to a higher life.
Plainness of speech, of manners, and attire,
Attest the weaning of the Christian heart
From worldly pleasures, honors, and pursuits.

SAMUEL.

With such a fruitage, is the tree secure
From questioning inspired, and Truth's decree, —
"Cut, cut it down; why cumbereth it the ground?"
Is the heart's fealty to God and truth,
A Saviour's teachings and a Saviour's love,
Proclaimed, secured, made manifest to all,
When, long and earnest cogitation o'er,

Numbered the plaits, the front's true curve secured,
And the just elevation of the crown, —
The *bonnet*, — raven black or sober drab,
In all its aspects, gives expression true
To what the aggregated wisdom deems
A fitting covering for the *friendly* head?

JEREMIAH.

What says the discipline?

SAMUEL.

And has the law —
The gospel law, the law by love fulfilled —
And the blessed ministry of the daily cross
Done all their work, their highest triumph found,
When singularity of diction (called,
By strange misnomer and assumption bold,
Plainness of speech) is by a pronoun gained, —
Used all unlike the erring world around, —
And saying "*John*" instead of "*Mr.*" Smith?

JEREMIAH.

And does thee* doubt the discipline?

SAMUEL.

'Twere well

Thus to conform in *number*, if the *case*,
In cases numberless, were not so oft
Objectionable; when the objective case,
Supreme above its banished bróthers twain,
Objective, nominative, possessive reigns.

JEREMIAH.

We must, thee knows, to discipline conform.

SAMUEL.

Sad the condition of the man who lives
A stranger to the beauty of the cross, —
That "daily dying" which gives daily life, —
And who for this in forms and creeds and rules
Seeks substitution. Light and love and life

---

* Note B.

Are fled; and, rapt in worldliness, he seeks
In forms, the fossils of departed life,
To win the right to bear the Christian name,
And find a Christian's refuge and reward.
Creeds, metaphysics of a bigot brain,
And rules and forms, — the sole vitality
Of corporate existence, — hold the place
Of instant ministering 'from Wisdom's fount,
And make the mystery of the Spirit's power
A thing of garb and grammar.

JEREMIAH.

Thee's doing discipline a grievous wrong.

SAMUEL.

Then let the discipline the wrong requite;
And, when thy friend is under dealing brought
For dealing honestly with it and thee,
'Twere well, methinks, to give him in the dock*
The fellowship of our esteemed Friend
Benajah Luvchink, — him thou knowest deemed,

---

* Note C.

Among the weighty, weightiest.   In his walk
And conversation, manners and address,
He is an incarnated discipline,
All fearless standing at each month's broadside
Of *queries** from the discipline discharged.
But recently, he stood within the yard
Where his new ship is building.   Long discourse
He held with Thomas, master-workman there,
Touching the merits of a mighty stick
To form the stern-post.   Sorrowing, he had seen
A small defect, and had the master called
The spot to view, and talk the matter o'er.
Pending the question, lo, the hour arrived
When Friend Benajah must to meeting go.
He went, and duly greeted all the Friends;
And then, with features fitted to the place,
His body seated and his mind composed.
No *movement* broke the solemn stillness there :
We passed in silence the accustomed hour.
The extended hand the parting signal gave,
And Friend Benajah to his home repaired.

---

* Note D.

His frugal meal despatched, with quickened step
He sought the timbered yard; and, on the oak
Whose imperfections had his trouble made,
He found the master seated; who at once
Thus his employer greeted: " It will do."
" It will, no doubt," Benajah quick replied :
" *I've thought about it all our meeting-time.*" *

JEREMIAH.

Thrift is a virtue in Benajah's eyes,
And thoughtful prudence is the ministry
By which it lives.

SAMUEL.

   Thrift, thus exalted high,
Claims its full share of homage; and the hour
We to devotion give may well be spent
In solemn cogitation how to save
A stern-post from the wood-pile.

---

* Note E

JEREMIAH.

                                    Thee is wrong
Thus to decry the testimony strong
Of weighty Friends now gone to their reward, —
Barclay and Fox and Pennington and Penn, —
And hosts of others, faithful to the end.*

SAMUEL.

Spare me thy music : no occasion calls
For this display of tuneful exhortation.
Thou art not now upon the rising-seat.
Murray and Goold (both weighty Friends), well
        known
At Haverford, at Providence as well,
Have taught that English grammar is the art
Correctly to express by speech or pen
The English language.   Pass the syntax by ;
The tax too great the chronic sin to cure
Of daily violations of the laws
Of speech, in case and number, numberless.

---

* Note F.

But speech has other laws, — by nature formed,
By wisdom perfected, and use ordained.
By these, when reason clothes the thought in
    words,
When feeling to its gushings utterance gives,
When passion flashes and when mercy pleads,
And indignation thunders its behest,
All speech is governed; and each living word
Flies on its embassy of weal or woe,
Winged by the potency of utterance clear,
A graceful manner, and an earnest soul;
And, by an intonation richly robed,
Like beauty by the sculptor's chisel traced.

JEREMIAH.

Thy words, my friend, sound strangely to my ear.

SAMUEL.

Dost miss the twang conventional, the tone
Which, by some instinct or some custom strange,
So oft our public ministrations make
Revolting violations of the rules   ·
Which nature, law, and usage have ordained?

How painful and how futile, when the voice
Ranges the gamut in a single word,
And touches every discord on the track!
How often exhortations are sent forth
With such negations strange in tone and speech
Of all propriety, that they become
Grating to hear, and impotent for good!
From such exhortings, neither said nor sung, —
Alike removed from poetry or prose, —
Impinging on the doubting, troubled ear
With sounds which bear no message to the brain,
When shall we be delivered?   Could I speak
With Cowper's tongue, I would, like Cowper,
        plead
With those who sacred supervision keep
O'er such as minister in sacred things,*
From ministrations such as these to save
The gatherings of our people.

JEREMIAH.

                'Twould be strange
To hear the speaking from our rising-seats,

---

* Note G.

Like recitations in a public school,
Or social readings at our quiet homes,
Or hireling sermons from the pulpit sped,
Without that solemnizing, measured tone
Which marks its coming from a sacred source.

SAMUEL.

Which marks its coming from a sacred source!
Did the Great Teacher speak the word of life
With a rude sing-song, indolent as rude?
When Felix trembled, and when Athens heard
From Paul the message of the Prince of Peace,
Did he, the noblest soul that ever bore
That message to an erring, suffering world,
Dole out his reasonings awful and sublime,
Like strop-man at his improvised bazaar,
Like show-man with his stereotyped harangue,
Or half-crazed preacher at camp-meeting found?

JEREMIAH.

The matter weighty, why the manner heed?
He who the Leader follows cannot pause
To give his thought to utterance and tone.

SAMUEL.

Such was *his* answer, whose discordant tones
Revolting fell upon the startled ear,
And closed all access to the mind and heart.
He who with quickened thought, by love inspired,
Burns with a message to my waiting soul,
Fails in his high commission, if it comes
With such environment of tone and speech,
That sense and taste in joint rebellion rise,
And bar its entrance.

JEREMIAH.

         Surely, Truth Divine
Needs not the foreign aid of ornament.*

SAMUEL.

Spare me, Friend Austen, this unmeaning cant.
Truth, Truth Divine, whenever she commands
The ministration of the human thought,
Claims all that thought and reason can impart

---

* Note H.

To give her word attractiveness and power.
Would that the teachings of the Holy Word,
So oft recited, and which often make
Of our prelections the potential part, .
And all that "Highest Wisdom" may supply
Of exhortation, could an utterance find
Like that which listening crowds enamoured hear,
When SHAKSPEARE through the gifted *Kemble*
  speaks,
Dewey interprets COLERIDGE's* mystic page,
And *Shaw,** with genius kindred to their own,
Unveils the beauties of the BROWNINGS' song!
Shall elocution lavish all its skill,
In making patent to the common thought,
The gifts of genius to the world of mind?
Leaving to rude, untutored tone and speech
The words of sacred prophecy and song,
The matchless teachings of the Saviour's lips,
Paul's earnest letters and his speech sublime.
When he the gifted, he the silver-tongued,
The elocutionist without a peer,

---

* Note I.

Speaks to the people of the peerless one,
And bids the Father of his Country hail,*
How apt each word! its utterance how clear!
How rich and full of meaning every tone!
While grace of attitude and motion join
With the mute eloquence of eye and face
To crown the speaker AUTOCRATOR there.

JEREMIAH.

Thy speech is strange: I do not understand.
What names are these of which I hear thee speak?
Shakspeare and Coleridge, Browning, Dewey, Shaw,
Kemble, and Autocrat, — are they public Friends?

SAMUEL.

Some to the public are not quite unknown;
Although the liberty of pen and speech
Came in no shape the discipline approves, —
Certificate, in form, and duly signed,
Of meetings, *yearly, quarterly, select,*
Monthly, preparative, for *sufferings,* †

---

* Note J.   † Note K.

The right conferring on the favored one
To be a teacher to his fellow-man.

JEREMIAH.

Thee spoke of Shakspeare, and of Brownings' *song*.
Songs and their writers cannot hold a place
Approved and cherished in the thoughts of Friends.

SAMUEL.

Then let us banish from our hearts and homes
The Judean records.   Let us quick disown
Whittier,* the gifted son of song, whose lays ·
Have the true lyric ring; and who, in lines
As touching and as sweet as Burns ere sung,
Pays heartfelt homage to his brother-bard, —   ·
Scotland's dear minstrel, of the world beloved.
Rememberest thou when we were at a school,
A half a century or more ago,
Founded, endowed, and managed by the Friends
Of Massachusetts?   Elam was its friend.
He gave his money; and, a richer gift,

---

* Note L.

He gave his books, — collection rich and rare :
But, ere from Elam's island-home they reached
The academic hall, the Elam books
Must an expurgatory process know
By the stern censorship that kept the gate
To bar the entrance of all hurtful things ;
And, when the longed-for treasures were revealed,
The " *British Poets* " had been ostracized,
And SHAKSPEARE *minuted* contraband,* and—sold !

JEREMIAH.

" Judean records ; " " Whittier, gifted son ; "
" Scotland's   dear   minstrel ; "   " Shakspeare ; "
    " British Poets," —
Why speak of these ?   For what they have to do
With Friends, or with the tidings from abroad,
I understand not.   I was moved to say,
That 'twas with apprehension and alarm
I heard the rumor of the mournful change
Which makes our customs, bulwarks of the church,
By which we stand distinctive and select, —

---

* Note M.

Plainness of speech, of manners, and of dress, —
No longer hold unquestioned and revered
Their high position.   Plainly can I see,
With thee these apprehensions have no place,
My anxious fears no sympathy.   How long,
This overturning spirit· unrestrained,
Shall we retain our form, so highly prized,
Of silent worship?

SAMUEL.

                    . Worship has no form.
To sit, to kneel, to stand, to speak, to think,
Determine not the spirit's attitude.
Speech may be silver, silence may be gold,
And both be sounding or unsounding brass.
We dust our knees ; but no repentant dust
Dims the bright polish of our self-conceit.
A "tinkling cymbal" were a sure relief
From drowsy Silence, as she slowly moves
Her leaden sceptre o'er a slumbering band,*
Convened and ranged in form and order due.

---

* Note N.

JEREMIAH.

Then what is worship ?

SAMUEL.

       Tell me what is not,
When on the bosom of the Infinite
The spirit rests submissively and meek;
When the heart finds its daily meat and drink —
Its will subdued, its wishes, hopes, desires,
Moving in union with the Will Divine —
In daily homage to the Eternal Love.
All work of God, commanded or allowed,
Is worship, when, by right divine, the soul
Joins in the sympathy that wakes the harps
Of choirs angelic round the eternal throne.

JEREMIAH.

Remember what the Sacred Record says :
" Be still, O man ! and know that I am God."

SAMUEL.

Man may " be still," and yet he may not " know."
Hast yet to learn that silence has no power

To grapple with the importunities
Somniferous, which, on soft-cushioned seats,
Bind and subdue the willing captives there?
Silence no charm or conjuration wields
To exorcise the demon of the world,
When he appears, companion unrebuked,
Of faces formal, elongate, and sad.
Silence may reign when at the chosen place
The people meet collectively to "wait
Upon the Lord." Some wait awhile, and then
To Somnus quietly their homage yield,
And, by a nod, unconscious worship pay.
Some wait a moment; and, when all is still,
They hear the whistle of the railroad train, —
Railroad "Celestial," * — whose conductor, full
Of complaisance and prudence, has prepared
A car for those who in a quiet way
A little work " terrestrial " would perform, —
Accommodation great for those who think
The whole *first day* too large a sacrifice.
They mount; and now there's sterner work in
        hand
Than comes of single stern-posts. On they speed,

---

* Note O.

And build the thick-ribbed ship from stem to stern;
Launch her, and load, and send her on her way,
And bring her back, a golden harvest won.
Thus " some renew their strength " by balmy
    sleep;
And some " mount upwards " as on golden wings,
Beholding visions of increasing gain.
Thus these to Mammon, those to Morpheus, bow:
'Tis thus they " wait," and thus they are " re-
    newed."
Better the " long-drawn aisle and fretted vault,"
The painted window and the vestured priest,
The swelling organ and the hireling song;
Better the Liturgy's unvarying sound;
Better the Mass misguided masses seek;
Better the closet's deeply studied lore,
With unimpassioned utterance discharged;
Better the rude, unmeaning dance and song,
The Shaker's safety-valve for false restraint;
Better the harmonies of flute and horn
Heard at Moravian worship; better far
The songs and shoutings and the loud amens
At crowded vestries and camp-meetings heard.

JEREMIAH.

Our speech and silence are alike condemned.

SAMUEL.

Nor speech nor silence are by me condemned.
The spirit's homage to the Infinite Good,
By adoration or obedience paid,
Is worship, waiting : they who worship wait,
And they who truly wait are worshippers.
Forms are but servitors to lift the gates
To let the King of glory enter in, —
The needful aids of doubting, struggling faith.

JEREMIAH.

Wouldst rouse *our* sleepers by an organ-peal ?
By forms liturgic keep the world at bay ?
And help the halting by a painted wall ?
Where, then, our high distinctions ?   Where our
        claim
To nearest access to the Infinite Mind
In silent waiting ?   Where the higher claim
Of instant guidance by the Master's hand·
In every act of prophecy and praise ?

SAMUEL.

Oh ! spare the " high distinction," — spare the
    " claim ; "
The bigot's solace and the sectarist's boast.
Where our distinction in. the eyes of Him
Who seeth, knoweth, loveth, keepeth all ?
The mind of God is known to them alone
Who do the Father's will.   To him unknown
All geographic, all sectarian bounds, —
His tender mercies over all his works.
The life of God within the soul of man
Feeds not upon the interpretation dim
Of music's strain, though Handel press the keys ;
Of highest plastic or pictorial art
Of SANZIO * or of BUONAROTTI * born ;
Or iterated flow of solemn speech,
Echoed by swelling dome or pillared aisle.
God is his own interpreter ; and, when
The Sacred Presence † fires the waiting soul,
Or be there speech or silence, there is known

The full fruition of immortal joy.
Holy the flame that on the altar glows,
By fire celestial kindled and supplied.
Presumptuous man, with sacrilegious hand,
Would fain its sacred heat and light apply
To gild and vivify his lifeless forms :
Device Promethean* to give his work
The heavenly impress of the life divine.
Man in his manliness, when reason's light
Shines with the radiance of its Primal Source,
Reigns autocrat within his own domain.
His high prerogatives by God bestowed,
God will, himself, acknowledge and protect.
'Twere well to heed the teachings of the rule
Rhetorical, by ancient wisdom penned,
For those who dared the heights of epic song :
The gods should never on the earth appear,
Except their work be godlike.†   Let us not   .
Place on our rules and forms conventional
The image and the superscript divine.
The precepts of our fathers bear no seal
The wisdom of the children may not break.

---

* Note R.   † Note S.

Open to bold revision every form
Of marriage rite, of language, and of dress.
True to the inward life, we shall not need
The organ's peal or hireling's speech or song
To lead our spirits in the solemn act
Of public worship. We shall ever find
Nearness of access to the Infinite Mind,
When silently we wait; in every act
Of exhortation, prayer, or praise, shall know
The instant guidance of the Master's hand.

JEREMIAH.

Farewell! To-day the men's committee meet,
Appointed in the case of Thomas Swift,
Charged with a serious breach of discipline,
In having at his house, for instant use,
A stringèd instrument, piano called.*

SAMUEL.

Farewell! and, when you deal with Thomas Swift,
Remember good King David had the same
At home, and in the holy temple too.

---

* Note T.

NOTES.

NOTES.

NOTE A.

" That leads to bewilder, and dazzles to blind."

My change in Beattie's beautiful line is no improvement. Had the rhythm conformed, I should have left it unchanged. I allude to it, that the confession of the plagiarism may, as in other cases of larceny, abate the punishment.

NOTE B.

" And does thee doubt the discipline?"

I allow Friend Jeremiah to speak after his own fashion. This chronic form of diseased speech seems to admit of no cure. Friends should legalize it by having it recognized in the next editions of Murray and Goold.

NOTE C.

" 'Twere well, methinks, to give him in the *dock*."

Webster defines a *dock* to be "the place where a criminal stands in court." Such a place has but a figurative existence in monthly-meeting proceedings under the discipline code; but such proceedings sometimes put people in a *tight place.*

NOTE D.

" Of queries from the discipline discharged."

I hope, when the time shall come for our code to be revised, that the matter contained in the queries will be changed from its interrogatory to a declaratory form. It is, no doubt, highly proper that the *sleeping-in-meeting* business should have attention certainly as often as once a month; but it would, I think, save some hard straining for answers, and be quite as effective, if in place of the usual query, " Are Friends careful to abstain from sleeping in meeting? " a declaration should be solemnly made, that *no person, indulging in the habit of sleeping during the hour of worship, has any right to a seat in an assembly convened for that purpose.* And so of other matters contained in the queries.

NOTE E.

" I've thought about it all our meeting-time."

Founded on fact. We might probably multiply the number of Benajahs, were all as candid.

NOTE F.

It is not in my power to introduce the musical notation to describe Friend Jeremiah's style of speaking.

At present, we are not, at *our* school, initiated into the mysteries of *do, re, me,* &c.; so I cannot in the text give any·idea of this (to me) most revolting *sing-song.* It is astonishing ·that persons of fair intellectual attainments, who everywhere else, and at all times beside, speak with a natural tone, and in a simple and unaffected manner, should, the moment they open their lips on the *rising-seat,* ignore all the laws of elocution and common sense. What would be thought of a member of the first class in reading, at Providence School, if he should read an extract from Macaulay or Milton after the manner so often presented to him from the high-seat? If the training of the school is ever of any value, it certainly must be when its recipient takes the position of a public·religious teacher. He has no right to set aside the rules by which, through all time, the spoken word has been rendered effective. If he would give his message its greatest force, he must send it forth with all those accompaniments which the world has recognized as the laws of successful utterance. Two reasons may be given for this almost universal habit: I mean, of course, among the ministers of our society. The first is, that it is easy. It requires very much less effort to send forth our words in this " rude sing-song," than it does to give them the emphasis and intonation a perfect elocution requires. Believing this, I have ventured to use the word *indolent* in connection with this habit. But, when Jeremiah speaks of the tone which marks the sacred source of the words, he makes a declaration of a fact widely existing among us; and this is the second reason. I cannot here speak as I think the subject requires, of this deeply-seated but most absurd and most unfortunate notion. The term I have used may seem undignified, but it is not improper. It is nothing but a notion to believe that there can be any peculiar solemnity attached to an intonation which sets at defiance all the laws of speech.

It it but just for me to say, that all our public speakers do not thus offend.

The members of the Providence School often hear, at the school and in the city, speaking from Providence Friends, the manner of which does them no discredit as official advisers in the government of two of the highest educational institutions of the State of Rhode Island.

The gifted young woman, who sometimes visits us from Southern Massachusetts, has been, when I have heard her, as perfect in her intonation as she was sweet in her tones and correct and elegant in her language. Her exhortations lose none of their solemnity by the classical purity of their language, or the truthful modulation of her musical periods.

One other I would name; and he, too, is from the same section of country. That young man, whose voice I have often heard, and always heard with profit and delight, at our yearly meetings, has risen superior to that pressure of custom and tradition which has led astray so many of our ministers. Of all our public speakers, I have heard no one who comes to his work with so large a share of the proprieties of speech. It is evident that he regards it as a duty to give to his ministrations all the aid that is to be derived from purity of language, an easy and graceful manner, a clear enunciation, and an intonation in harmony with the meaning of his words. I may be allowed, in close, to remark, that it is to be hoped that the example of these public Friends from New Bedford and Nantucket will not be without its influence in the society.

Note G.

" Could I speak
With Cowper's tongue, I would, like Cowper, plead."

Hear how Cowper·pleads : —

" From such apostles, O ye mitred heads!
Preserve the church; and lay not careless hands
On skulls that cannot teach, and will not learn."

Note H.

"Needs not the foreign aid of ornament."

Another larceny; but I cannot now say from whom. It is a line Jeremiah would be likely to remember.

Note I.

I name the public readers I have heard. The kinswoman of the Siddons must, I suppose, be allowed the highest place. Mary Dewey, daughter of the Doctor, is a fine reader. Hood is more than ever Hood, when she stands interpreter. The reading of the "Ancient Mariner" came nearly up to the highest standard. Emily Shaw is the daughter of the Hon. John Shaw of Nantucket. In scenes of deep pathos, she excels both the others. The reading of the death of Jo, from Dickens's "Bleak House," was a performance I have never heard equalled. The minutest shades of thought and feeling are developed in the light of her clear, full, distinct utterance and faultless intonation, and by a corresponding expression of feature, which is the most attractive and astonishing characteristic of this gifted lady. The versatility of her powers enables her to give with equal and almost unequalled truthfulness and effect the coarse originality of Toby Belch, and the exquisite tenderness and deep contrition of Mildred Tresham : —

"I — I was so young!
Beside, I loved him, Thorold — and I had
No mother — God forgot me — so I fell."

These graces of delivery I regard as qualities of the highest value. To despise and reject them is to cast away the most effective aids to our public religious teachings.

Note J.

"And bids the Father of his Country hail."

This line is not mine; at any rate, not the whole of it. As it stands, it well answers my purpose; for it shows

that I am speaking of Edward Everett. Emerson says
of him, that he 'is the greatest elocutionist of the age.

NOTE K.

This list of meetings is almost as difficult to versify as
Homer's Catalogue, which is such a puzzle to the
translators; but I believe I have named them all. The
meeting *For Sufferings* was so called, in England, because one of its most important duties is to extend the
care and aid of the society in cases where suffering follows an adherence to duty. It is expected that all
writings in reference to the principles and usages of the
society will be submitted to this meeting before publication. Therefore it is that the writer of this little book
is an offender, should there not be an offending line
in it.

NOTE L.

> " Whittier, the gifted son of song, whose lays
> Have the true lyric ring."

I know not what the booksellers say; but my belief
is, that the poems of Whittier have had a more exten-
sive and powerful influence upon the minds of the people
than the writings of any other American poet. He is
the New-England Lyrist. He has shown us the potency
of the lyric power, and how effective it is when wielded
in the support of freedom and truth. For the first time

in its history, the Society of Friends has produced a
poet; and not only produced, but pardoned. The lyrist
having made his way into our homes, the lyre must soon
follow. The painter has also made a lodgment. He
who looks upon the beautiful painting by Bradford of
Fairhaven, now on exhibition at the National Gallery
in New York, with the slightest ability of appreciation,
will not only feel that the production of such a work is
a well-directed exercise of man's highest and most
enlarged ability, but that the taste that it educates and
gratifies is one that is intended by Him who thus endowed us to be cultivated and enjoyed. I hope I shall
be pardoned for using the word "lyrist," as meaning not
only the singer, but the maker, of the lyric.

Note M.

> " The ' British Poets ' had been ostracized,
> And Shakspeare *minuted* contraband, and — sold ! "

Fact: so says a Friend who has seen the *minute.*
This was not, however, directly a society matter. It
was the Board of Friendly Trustees who decided that
the Library of the Friends'. Academy must not contain
the dangerous volumes. Whittier was not a member
of the Board.

Note N.

Young wrote, — .

> " Her leaden sceptre o'er a slumbering world ; " —

and he wrote it so nearly right for me, that I could not resist the temptation to appropriate it, with a trifling change.

Considering this, and the several other lines which a pretty retentive memory, joined with some small ability of appreciation, have enabled me to work into the homely texture of my verse from the writings of the poets, it must be allowed that the colloquy has some good lines in it.

Note O.

> "Railroad ' Celestial,' whose conductor, full
> Of complaisance and prudence, has prepared."

Hawthorne has given us a striking description of the Celestial Railroad. According to his account, arrangements have been made for carrying on nearly every kind of terrestrial traffic in these cars.

Note P.

> " Of Sanzio or of Buonarotti born."

Raphael and Michael Angelo. The rhythm made it difficult to use the more commonly known names of these great men.

Note Q.

> " And when a sense of sacred presence fires," —

wrote the great and good Dr. Johnson.

NOTE R.

"Device Promethean, to give his work
The heavenly impress of the life divine."

Man is ever prone to imitate the Titan, and lay hold
of the heavenly fire to animate his own handiwork.
How often is our own ecclesiastical machinery regarded
as holding its life through the direct agency of heaven.

NOTE S.

" The gods should never on the earth appear,
Except their work be godlike."

Blair states Aristotle's rule thus : " Never permit a
god to appear but on an occasion worthy of a god."

NOTE T.

" A stringèd instrument, piano called."

Notwithstanding the earnestness and eloquence of
Samuel, Jeremiah is thinking more about removing that
stringed instrument from Friend Swift's house, or dis-
owning him for keeping it there, than about weightier
matters. We have many of these mint, anise, and
cumin members. As a matter of fact, I may as well
state that Thomas was disowned. The time, I believe,
is not far distant, when Shakspeare will not be banished
from the library, or the piano from the parlor.

9783337408343